Struggles for Freedom

D0913315

Struggles
for
Freedom

AN ANTHOLOGY OF MULTICULTURAL EXPERIENCES

DONNA L.CLOVIS

BRYANT AND DILLON PUBLISHERS, INC.
ORANGE, NEW JERSEY

Library of Congress Cataloging in Publication Data
Clovis, Donna L., 1957
1.Struggles for Freedom 2.Multicultural 3.History
(A Bryant and Dillon Book)
CIP # 94-78465
ISBN 0-9638672-2-9

Printed in the United States of America
September 1994
10 9 8 7 6 5 4 3 2 1

Dedicated to my family...

Contents

I am free

beyond the boundaries of a country which attempts to capture

my soul and spirit

Laws dictate, I am nothing

without rights

without being

I am free

for no man can incarcerate my spirit

It soars like the Phoenix in my heart eternal

I am free.

INTRODUCTION

Struggles For Freedom, An Anthology of Multicultural Experiences is a collection of personal interviews, short stories, and poetry about various peoples and countries who find themselves struggling for freedom. The personal interviews and short stories are real and have been compiled and transcribed over a period of ten years. Interviews have been conducted with high school students, college students, teachers, professors, engineers, beauticians, farmers, steel workers, and others from different countries to give a more informative and rounded look at how environments shape and affect people. I have composed the poetry for each country based upon the emotional experiences and stories of the people interviewed.

You will encounter many viewpoints and strong feelings. You will learn about geography, beauty, foods, customs, conflicts, and freedom. We can learn much about each other and other cultures by talking and exchanging ideas. You will learn how the theme of freedom plays an integral part in the lives of people throughout the world. You will learn much about the changing faces and cultures by these short stories and interviews.

It is hoped that our world will finally realize that we are drawn together by the same needs and feelings, and there is a continued need to communicate and understand other cultures as the face of our society changes day by day.

CHAPTER 1   HAITI

REPATRIATON

Thought I heard voice of North Star ringing

freedom

Ocean whispers hope

Darkness, night sings lullabies of dreams

treading waters, bobbing government decisions

waiting

Shipbottom rowboats, cold and frigid

Thought I heard voice of North Star ringing

freedom

Wanna new home

Haiti is so far away...

Haiti

Population 6.3 million

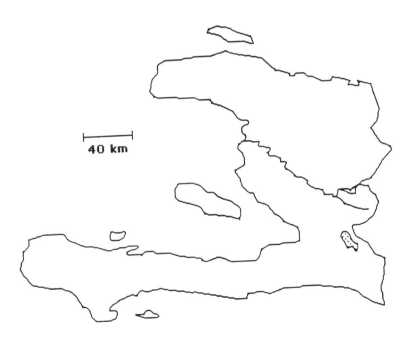

JOURNEY TO FREEDOM

The only way out of Haiti was by boat. It was a very dark evening, about midnight when the moon shone itself milky white, that we entered the choppy seas. I hated to leave my homeland, but knew the troubles had escalated. People were killed and their land and homes taken away. It was I and my wife who hid ourselves within the depths of the boat. We would risk a better life than reside in a land of hatred.

We were nervous and afraid. Several boats were loading people at the same time. It was difficult to keep quiet, for there came a time when there were too many people in the boat. Some started screaming and shouting for their loved ones to come on. Others fell into the cold, gasping waters of the sea as we left the shore.

We were leaving our families. How I wanted to bring my mom and dad, but I was afraid they were too old for the voyage. Nonetheless, I felt feelings of remorse and excitement at the same time.

The turbulent waters started to make some of the people on board very sick, including my wife. I tried to comfort her. It was difficult because the boat was overcrowded and there was no room to move or walk.

Suddenly we heard screams and cries for help! The neighboring boat had split causing all of the people on board to spill into the icy sea. We wanted to help, but couldn't help. We had too many people on our boat too. The cries died out shortly as the turbulence and monstrous sound of the ocean, swallowed up the dead.

Sleep crept upon all of us that night and we were awakened the next morning by the brightness of the sun. My wife complained of the hunger pains she began to feel in her stomach. I comforted her with all that I could, a hug.

Kim, from Haiti, takes a break from her work at a local flea market.

For days, our boat lay afloat upon the high seas. My mind reminisced of the beautiful fields that I used to run through as a child in Haiti. The wonderful tropical flowers and the fresh fruits which squeezed their juices freely for us, were just a memory.

Finally, we reached the coast of Florida. My heart cried, Freedom! Although my body was dirty and weak from the voyage, I jumped up and shouted in the overcrowded ship. We had to wait on the sea for two days before we were allowed on shore. We were some of the lucky ones. Our ship had not been turned back to Haiti like the others arriving after us.

I embraced my wife with hope. We have been given the gift of life, a second time. Freedom!

EXCERPTS FROM AN INTERVIEW

Donna Clovis: Tell us about Haiti's History.

Mrs. Pierre: We have a very rich history. There was a large castle fortress built at the top of the mountain range in Haiti in the 1800's. It is called Citadelle Lafierrier. It represents all of the hope and dreams of the Haitian people. It protected Haiti from the French, and it stands tall and high as Haiti's symbol.

Mr. Pierre: Haiti was the first country of Black slaves that successfully revolted against the colonists and won. We became independent.

Mrs. Pierre: This castle shows our Haitian spirit, not to give up. We believe things will be better one day in Haiti, if we have good spirit and hope. I just think Haiti wants to solve the problems alone, without outside help.

DC: What makes Haiti beautiful?

Mrs. Pierre: It is a place where the clouds touch the tops of mountains. The word Haiti means Mountains because there's so many. Most of the island is mountainous. There are palm trees, flowering trees of pink and red blossoms, and warm summer winds that whisper through the trees. Some of the mountains are quite rugged and difficult to climb.

Mr. Pierre: Ah, and the open air markets where we buy fresh foods like mango and guava fruit.

Mrs. Pierre: I can still taste the fresh water from the coconuts after it's just broken open.

Mr. Pierre: Because the weather is so good and warm, we can always eat meals outside beneath the vine and palm tree, listening to the birds and enjoying good family talk.

DC: Where did you live in Haiti?

Mr. Pierre: We owned a very small farm about 20 kilometers outside of the capital, Port-au-Prince. We didn't have machines to farm with so we used digging sticks and machetes to do our planting.

DC: What languages do you speak?

Mr. Pierre: Creole. It is a form of an African language and French, but it is only spoken, never do we write it. Creole was created during slavery.

Mrs. Pierre: The rich people learn French. That is the written language of Haiti, but many people do not know how to read and write. It is not so important because farming is the way of life.

Mr. Pierre: Creole and French are not the same language. They are very different. So when Haitian people come to America and learn English, they become people of three languages.

DC: What can I expect to see culturally in Haiti?

Mr. Pierre: You must visit the mural paintings of the Episcopal Cathedral of the Holy Trinity in Port-au-Prince. The murals were painted by some of the most famous Haitian artists. One famous artist is Hector Hippolyte. His works are beautiful.! Something you must see with your eyes.

Mrs. Pierre: It seems so strange that our country is so poor and can make such strong cultural work like art.

DC: If you could sum up your feelings about Haiti in one word, what would you say?

Mrs. Pierre: Wonderful...

Mr. Pierre: Come visit!

TRY THIS! A TASTE FROM OUR CULTURE ..

Fried Yam Chips (Haitian)

Ingredients:
1 lb yam
Salt to taste
4C cooking oil

Method:
1. Peel the yam, then slice it into paper-thin slices.
2. Drop the slices into very hot oil.
(This should only be done by an adult)
3. When the slices start to curl, take them out and drain them on paper towels. Sprinkle them with salt while still hot.

CHAPTER 2   BOSNIA

THE CAMPS

Videotape, society's secret eye

peering into the soul of Sarajevo

In her bosom rests Hitler's heart, pumping strong

Human blood spills into the seas...

Her atrocities mass to the heavens

Innocent dead flesh offend God's nose

and shock the world.

Yugoslav Federation

Population 17.1 million

100 km

HOMELAND

We used to live in the city of Dubrovnik. It was once a medieval jewel of white marble overlooking a calm sea. Our port city was filled with seven palaces of ancient kings and jewels and fifty-seven monuments depicting events of past history. In Sarajevo, you could visit an Oriental Institute which housed old documents in every Asian dialect and tongue. Or visit the town library to read century old archives. Several hundred mosques of unique architecture decorated the mountains, forests, and valleys.

Sometimes when I close my eyes, I can still smell my mother's roast dumplings, sauerkraut, and soups ooze beneath the kitchen doors outside where we used to play.

We are Croatians. There were about five million of us living in the area that used to be called Yugoslavia. Other people called Serbs and Muslims live there too. We used to live together in harmony and peace until two years ago. That's when we broke free from Communism and the Soviet Union. Then something crazy happened. Each group wanted their own land and state government. Fighting broke out and continues as I speak.

Then detention camps were formed in Bosnia and Croatia where thousands of Muslims have been taken and tortured. Horrors of starvation are rampant throughout the camps and thousands have died. The Serbs believe in something called, ethnic cleansing. It is a racist policy which allows the destruction and killing of Croat and Muslim people. It is a sad and unfair law. So many of our friends and relatives have died. Some reports say as many as 200,000 people on all sides are dead and 36,000 children are missing. Yet, despite obvious hardships, the beliefs of our people remain firm. We are committed to forming a Democratic system.

Ivan and his father from Bosnia share smiles during their interview.

The rewards of freedom and progress are worth the sacrifices. And with each sacrifice, will come prosperity.

I just hope peace and prosperity come soon to Bosnia and Sarajevo. And I can once again smell a roasted holiday goose and play in the peaceful forests of the countryside.

Soon.

EXCERPTS FROM AN INTERVIEW

Donna Clovis: So, Ivan, you come from Bosnia. How did you get to the United States?

Ivan: I'am here for only one year. I come to the United States as an exchange student to study.

DC: How old are you?

Ivan: I'am eighteen. I'am a senior in an American school.

DC: What do you think of American schools?

Ivan: They are fun. I like it because the students are very friendly and help me. I like to study here because there isn't the noise from the war. Some children can not go to school because of the war.

DC: What is it like living in a country at war?

Ivan: Of course, it is terrible. You must be careful where you go. Sometimes there is not enough food or water and the pains in your stomach are great. I've seen some friends die and I have an aunt who was killed too.

DC: Where is the rest of your family?

Ivan: They are in Bosnia. I have two sisters, a mother, and father. They have written to me twice.

DC: Are you afraid for them?

Ivan: Yes, they have moved now where there is less fighting.

DC: How do you feel about returning to Bosnia?

Ivan: I think, I must. I am not afraid. Maybe I can help my family. I will miss America. I have many good friends here. My friends are afraid for me. They don't want me to go back. They think I may be killed. But I belong to Bosnia. I want to go back.

DC: Do you think the war will end soon?

Ivan: I don't know. I hope. I hope because Bosnia is a very pretty place without war, but now it's terrible. I hope everyone can make peace.

DC: We wish you the best in everything, Ivan. Thank you.

TRY THIS! A TASTE FROM OUR CULTURE...

Fruit Soup

Ingredients:
one 1-lb can of dark sweet cherries in syrup
one 1-lb can of sliced peaches, drained
3 T lemon juice
2 C plain yogurt

Method:
1. Process the cherries with syrup, peaches, and lemon juice in a blender or food processor.
2. Stir in yogurt, then pour into 10 small bowls.

CHAPTER 3 COLUMBIA

COLUMBIAN PRINCESS

¡Hermanita mestiza, Merengue!

Little sister, dance Merengue!

Though sunlight pierces venetian blinds

slicing across your breast

through crimson dress, bleeding tears

Leaving scars of inequity-

Young voices martyred for freedom.

Nothing cuts our spirit

Merengue

¡Baile, mestiza!

Dance!

Columbia

Population 33.8 million

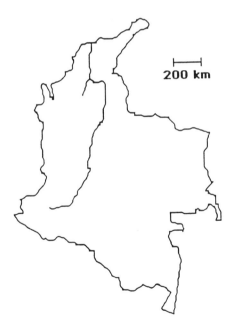

200 km

MERENGUE! LET'S DANCE AND CELEBRATE!

Buenos dias! Listen? Do you hear what I hear? The gentle beating of the drums in the background and merengue music? It's the beginning of our Carnival parade. A day of celebration and renewed spirit in our communities. There will be beautiful costumes of many colors, feathers, sequins, and mirrors. Some will wear masks of animals. This year's theme is flowers. It is a wonderful day for eating arroz con pollo (chicken with rice), dancing, singing, and watching the parade. What wonderful reasons do we have to celebrate now!

For in the 1980's, our country of Columbia had many, many problems. The guerilla movement and the drug cartels created much terroism. Buildings and homes were bombed and many of the innocent were killed. Drug traffickers killed many presidential candidates. They threatened to kill others who wanted to vote. There were outcries in the streets from the loss of loved ones. Yet, despite the violence, elections were finally held. Gaviria was elected.

Gaviria encouraged everyone to be peaceful. He even offered rights to some of the terrorists groups. Some accepted at first, others did not and caused more violence. Finally, Gaviria offered to be lenient to drug traffickers if they turned themselves in and stopped dealing drugs, and with success, the violence was stopped.

In the year 1990, we began to rewrite the constitution. We included all people from the population- Indians, former terrorists, and various party leaders. In 1991, our new constitution was ready to be implemented. Our country of Columbia now enjoys rule of law for everyone, no matter what they look like or if they are rich or poor.

Maria, Teresa, and Dona show off their costumes during their festival and parade.

So don't you think we have even more reason to be happy and celebrate our Carnival? Look at the marvelous headdresses of feathers coming down the street of the parade. Listen to the guitars and laughter. Watch the children play.

Baile! Dance! Enjoy!

EXCERPTS FROM AN INTERVIEW

Donna Clovis: Tell me a little about yourself.

Marie: My name is Maria Munoz Rodriguez and I am a professor at the National University in Bogota, Columbia.

DC: I noticed that you have two last names. Why?

Maria: It is a Spanish custom to have the last name of your father and mother. Munoz is the family name of my father and Rodriguez comes from my mother's family.

DC: I understand there are many varieties of people who live in Columbia. Describe your heritage.

Marie: I am called Mestizo. That's a mixture of Spanish and Indian. There are Blacks, Indians, Whites, and Mulattos that live in Columbia. Mulatto means a mixture of Black and White. There's also a Black and Indian mixture. Yes, Columbia is filled with many varieties of people, but we are all Columbian.

DC: Describe Columbia.

Marie: It's a wonderful place. There are snowy mountains and large jungles. There is an active volcano and valleys and plains. Columbia is about the size of California and Texas together. And the temperature is wonderful too. It is warm in Bogota, where I come from. The animals are beautiful and so are the trees. My favorite animal is the

Toucan bird. It has such beautiful colors in its beak.

DC: What are your favorite foods?

Maria: Arroz con pollo, that's chicken and rice, and plantains. They look like bananas and we fry them and of course good Columbian coffee.

DC: If I were to visit Columbia, is there anything I would need to know?

Maria: Yes (smiling), don't yawn in public. It's impolite. And smile alot. Everyone likes that.

DC: Why have you come to the United States?

Maria: To pursue my studies in Science. I am here for two years and then I will go back to Bogota.

DC: It's been great talking with you! Thanks.

TRY THIS! A TASTE FROM OUR CULTURE

Corn Pone

Ingredients:
1 1/2 C cornmeal
3/4 C flour
3 t baking powder
2 eggs, well beaten
1/4 C margarine, melted
1C milk

Method:
1. Mix the dry ingredients and the liquid ones separately.
2. Combine the two, stirring just until moistened.
3. Pour into an 8-in. square greased pan and bake at 350° F
for 20 minutes.

CHAPTER 4 NATIVE AMERICA

SONG OF OUR FLIGHT

Quiet orange sunrise

White moonlight until

the white man came

Hooves thundered over our burial grounds

Buffalo slain

Villages deserted

Teepees were mounted upon canoes, floating on surging waters

We fled across the plain

Tern flickered in the blood of crimson sky

Shrill of hawks echo

Our hearts pulse along the river

looking for a new home

Drums beat forever in monotone night

Although feathers of my headdress have been cut by adversity

my bow and arrow sings

and my head rises above the clouds...

United States of America

Population 252.5 million

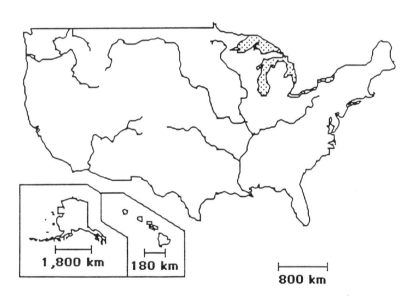

1,800 km

180 km

800 km

MAIZE LIFELINES

From where does life come? How shall it be sustained? The Great Spirit of the Sky has given us life and we are sustained by the maize (corn) from the ground. We are the Hopi residing upon the plateaus of the Midwest. In these desert plains, we have been blessed by the spirits of the distant and beautiful mountain. They have given us summer rains for growing corn.

Our ceremonies, dances, and way of life are centuries old. The clouds, the rain, the corn, passed on from generation to generation, never ending.

We plant our corn in the depths of the desert soil where it is moist and with the Home Dance, all gather in the village to pray and sing for rain. For the corn needs to grow and we, need to eat and survive. With the dance, in bright feathered headdresses, we beg the Kachina spirits for favor. Small boys are given gifts of bow and arrow and small girls are given gifts of Kachina dolls to keep. We must remember to pray for the rain.

When we have been blessed with rain, the corn will grow. With the wavering corn stalks upon the plains in September, we have been blessed and are ready to roast. A corn roast to celebrate our food is one of the most social Hopi events. A deep pit is dug into the belly of the earth by the strongest Hopi men. A fire is started at the base of the pit and covered with cornstalks, then corn, and more corn stalks. The stalks will create the moisture to steam and roast the corn. We cover the top of the pit and let the corn roast until the next morning.

The next morning, the corn is removed from the pit. Its steam rises steadily into the early morning sun, and with the steam, we Hopi believe that we are seeing the blessings from the cloud spirits.

Everyone helps to remove the husks from the corn and the ears are dried by gentle rays of sun. There's much excitement and happiness in the village. The maize is stored and preserved for the Hopi for the next years. Whenever we need food, we can place the corn in water and have a tasty meal.

So, from where does life come? How is it sustained? The Great Spirit of the Sky has given us life and we are sustained by the maize, the corn from the ground. We are the Hopi. Let us celebrate and sing an old song:

Yellow butterflies

Over blossoming virgin corn

With pollen painted faces

Chase one another in brilliant throng

Blue butterflies

Over the blossoming beans

With pollen painted faces

Chase one another in brilliant streams

Over the blossoming corn

Over the virgin corn

Wild bees hum

Over the blossoming beans

Over the virgin beans

Wild bees hum

Over your field of growing corn

All day shall hang the thunder clouds

Over the field of growing corn

All day shall come the rushing rain.

Sioux Indian women show their handmade costumes.

Little Deer shows her handmade necklace.

Little Coyote smiles at flea market.

EXCERPTS FROM AN INTERVIEW

Donna Clovis: What is your name, and what is its meaning?

Theresa: On the reservation, they call me Little Deer, but when I attend school, I am called Theresa. It's easier to have an American name when I go to school with American kids. My name, Little Deer, was given to me on the twentieth day after I was born. It is a Hopi custom to do that. I was named after my grandmother.

DC: The name of your tribe is Hopi. Where do you live?

Theresa: My family lives on a reservation in northeast Arizona. The countryside is pretty. It has mountains, deserts, and plains.

DC: Describe your village.

Theresa: We live in Pueblos in our village. They are made of adobe. Adobe is like brick or clay. The houses are built or stacked on top of each other. It bothers me when people think all Native Americans live in Teepees. That just isn't true. Some lived in wigwams made of sticks and mud or hogans or igloos where it is very cold. Native Americans always use nature to live. So, the Native American tribes can be very different. Even our languages are different.

DC: What languages do Native Americans speak?

Theresa: Many. There's Navajo, Lenape, Cherokee, Lakota, and Passamaquoddy. And they are so different from each other.

DC: What is your favorite ceremony or dance?

Theresa: I love the corn roast. That's because I love corn so much. The smells from the fire pit are so good. Corn is important to the Hopi people. It has kept us alive. My favorite corn is purple corn. It is called Kokoma.

DC: How old are you and what brings you to the east coast?

Theresa: I am nineteen and I am attending the university here. I want to become a doctor.

DC: Did you attend school on the reservation?

Theresa: No, I went to school outside the reservation with other American students. My family thought that I would get a better education there instead of on the reservation.

DC: Do you think they were right?

Theresa: Yes, there are more books and computers outside of the reservations and there are better opportunities as well.

DC: Was it difficult going to school with Americans?

Theresa: Sometimes. Sometimes people would make fun of you and ask you to do a rain dance or something, but that was all.

DC: What is the best thing about being a member of your tribe?

Theresa: That's a tough question. I think that the best thing is our family and the preservation of our people. The Hopi think that it is very important, never to forget our culture and ceremonies. No matter where I may live, I will never forget them.

DC: If you could say something to the children of the future, what would that be?

Theresa: Hmmmm. Be the best you can and don't forget where you came from.

TRY THIS! A TASTE FROM OUR CULTURE...

Succotash (Native American)

Ingredients:
one 10-oz can corn niblets
one 10-oz can kidney beans
one 10-oz can chickpeas
2C cooked wild rice
1/4C oil-and-vinegar dressing

Method:
1. Drain the cans of corn, beans, and chickpeas. Mix them with the rice.
2. Coat well with the salad dressing and serve in small bowls. This is also delicious as a filling for pita bread.

CHAPTER 5 SOUTH AFRICA

SOUTH AFRICA

Apartheid holds its victims in bondage

Rusted chains as necklaces dangle about inhabitants,

ignited in fury

Black against black, silhouette white

Upheavals moving toward change.

South Africa

Population 40.6 million

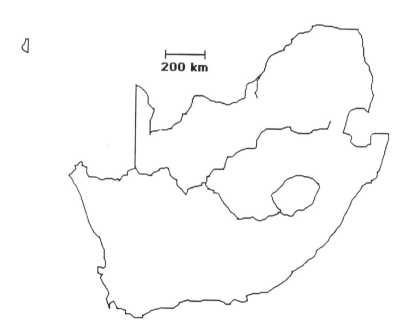

SOUTH AFRICA...A LOVE STORY

I stare into the icy night. The mighty river between our villages hardens. Moonbeams glisten upon its surface. Can we walk across its cold hatred to embrace the warmth of our love? As I glance into the darkness of the savannah, I wonder what he is doing and where he is, and why our lives in South Africa exist the way it does.My lover, our gardener, is a black man of the tribe of Zulu, and I am a woman with skin milky white and eyes of blue. Daily my lover comes to our estate to work and take care of the flowers, plants and many acres of ground and daily he must return to his own village where only Blacks can live. He travels nearly two hours by foot back and forth; in the morning with the crispness of the dawn and in the evening, with the quietness of dusk.

There are so many days that I long for him to stay, but our love is one that is secret. It is forbidden under the laws of Apartheid. Father doesn't know. Neither does mother or my brother. But I am twenty-six years old and old enough to know that I am desperately in love with a man who is a just and kind human being.

Tomorrow we shall leave South Africa and go to Canada.. He will leave first and I will leave the next day. This is the only way for us to be together. I've purchased the plane tickets for separate flights and have hidden them in the bottom of my bureau drawer. And I have removed all of my monies from bank accounts so we can have finances for our new start.

As the sun rises the next morning, I know he will be here, outside my bedroom window to get his plane ticket. My heart pulses nervously as I wait at my window. When he appears, I am relieved and a little frightened, for the journey ahead of us is long. We embrace and I give him the plane ticket for Toronto. He gently kisses my cheek and says, "I'll be there waiting for you. See you in three days.." He leaves.

The following day, it's my turn to leave. I follow without saying good-bye to my family. I leave a detailed note on the kitchen table. I will write them. I will call them when I get to Toronto.

As my plane ascends into the vast South African sky, I glance down and behold the beauty of a magnificent continent. The deep green forest, jungles, snow-tipped mountains, and deserts begin to mesh as one land form. I'll miss my walks in the savannah with the animals. I'll miss the seacoast, rivers, and grasslands, but I will never miss the hurt and hatred and death that has brewed in my homeland for many years.

I sleep for most of the trip, changing planes in London. My sleep is peaceful and I dream of a world of peace. When I think of him, I pretend he is near and say softly, "Close your eyes, for God's paintbrush is hidden from you now. Touch the softness of my color-less skin, and in the darkness know, we are the same."

When the flight has landed in Canada, I rush from the plane. Quickly I glance at everyone in the crowd. My eyes dart back and forth until...There he is! He sees me. We embrace with a strength I have never felt before...Love, Unity, and freedom!

EXCERPTS FROM AN INTERVIEW

Donna Clovis: How do you say Good Morning in South Africa?

Tounde: Oh, my dear, in so many ways. It depends on where you live. If you are Zulu, like me, you say sakubona. If you speak English, of course, it's hello.

Liz: If you are an Afrikaaner, it's golie more. Afrikaans comes from Dutch. More than half the people in South Africa speak it.

DC: Tell me more about the diversity of South Africa.

Tounde: There are so many different tribes. There are the Sotho, Tswana, Xhosa, Zulu and the Swazis. Among the whites, there are Irish, English and Scottish.

Liz: Also German and Dutch. The Coloureds are people who are intermixed with Whites and Blacks from the earlier settlements.

Tounde: We must not forget the Indians from India. Each group is culturally different and may speak their own language.

DC: Where do all of these people live?

Liz: Under Apartheid, everyone lives in their own separate towns and villages. They're called Homelands. Blacks and Whites may work together or for another, but everyday must travel back to the Homeland. I think though, since 1991 people can live wherever they want. The Land Areas Acts were done away with.

DC: Where do you live?

Liz: We live in Canada. We left South Africa five years ago during Apartheid. Under the law, we couldn't marry each other because I am White and Tounde is Black.

DC: Are you married now?

Liz: Yes. We were married in Canada.

DC: What are your favorite South African foods?

Tounde: Again, that depends on where you live, who you are and how much money you have. For example, rich Whites enjoy fresh beef and mutton, potatoes and vegetables. If you are poor or Black and live in the rural villages, you may eat mealie meal. That's a porridge of cornmeal. Sometimes it is cooked with vegetables and meat.

DC: Tell us about Apartheid.

Liz: It is a terrible law that segregates people according to color.

Tounde: There were many people jailed and killed because of it. Blacks wanted to be treated the same. At least now there is a movement toward a multiracial society.

DC: If the laws have changed, what do you think of people's attitudes towards people of a different race? Do you think they will automatically change?

Liz: Certainly not. I think it will take a long time for people to change their views. Look at the United States, some people are still racist in their hearts even though segregation is not practiced.

Tounde: I am very happy to see that the laws have been disbanded. At least there is some movement towards change. A step at a time is fine as long as there is progress.

DC: What do you think it will take for people to be equal there?

Tounde: They will need to get to know one another with an open mind. When people become friends and see that the feelings are the same, that we all bleed, we all live and we all die...Maybe we will be equal and find that we all are just human beings. Hopefully, we will find a way to help each other.

DC: Tell me about the African countryside. What do you miss?

Liz: The countryside is so beautiful. I miss the freedom of the animals to walk about.

Tounde: Also there's such a variety of climate. Africa has beautiful mountains with snow and tropical rainforests. It has the dry grassland and savannah. It can be very hot and it can be very cold depending on where you are. As I think now, I miss the music. The dancing of my Zulu tribe and the wonderful Storytellers who spoke bewitching tales late at night.

Liz: I miss my family. They write to us and I hope to see them for the first time since I left in a few months. They are coming to Canada.

DC: Are you happy with your decision to leave South Africa?

Liz: Yes, definitely. I have such a wonderful life with Tounde.

Tounde: And I agree.

A woman shows off her native costume and a map of Africa.

TRY THIS! A TASTE FROM OUR CULTURE

Akwadu (Africa)

Ingredients:
3 medium bananas
3 t margarine or butter
1/2 C orange juice
3 t lemon juice
1 C unsweetened shredded coconut

Method:
1. Preheat the oven to 350° F.
2. Peel and cut the bananas in half crosswise, then lenghtwise in half again. Arrange the bananas on a greased pie plate.
3. Dot the bananas with margarine or butter, then drizzle with the juices, and sprinkle the coconut on top.
4. Bake for 10-15 minutes, or until the coconut is golden.

CHAPTER 6 THE SOVIET REPUBLIC

TOPOGRAPHER

Splitting atom of discontent

explosive outcries

chaos shatters Earth-

quaking Genesis, government birth.

Land masses collide, then separate

Facial contours change as

Mapmaker carves new boundaries

Russia.

Russia

Population 147.4 million

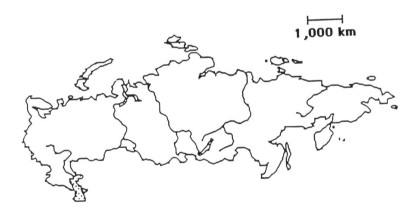

1,000 km

THE MEANING OF FREEDOM

"Zdravstvuyte! Come enter our home! Russian people love to have friends and guests, especially foreign ones. Take off your shoes and leave them at the door. Sit at our table and let's talk for awhile! Ahhh...You've brought such lovely flowers for us and vodka! What a fine expression of friendship!

So, how are things here? Well, as you know things have been in quite a bit of turmoil. We have had very few opportunities to make any decisions on our own without the help of the government. It is very hard to make decisions on our own. Now, why, yes, things have changed. For the better? I don't know. I really don't know. Many days I sit here by my window very pessimistic about the future. Maybe most Russian people are. Some of us long for the old way of life. I know, you Americans don't understand. How could you want a life under Communism? Don't you like freedom? I don't know. With freedom, there are new social values. With freedom there is inflation and unemployment. With freedom there is very little food. Is this good? Is this bad? Freedom has reduced the quality of our lives. Is this the price to pay for freedom?

Friendship is what keeps me going. Having kind people to share the day with us is what makes my life worth living. I'm seventy years old now. Maybe I am too old for new things. Maybe the young people can make freedom work. They have the energy and stamina. For me, each day gets more difficult to live. I've stopped all of my political participation. I can't help it. I'm too old and it's too hard.

Yes, I do live in the crown jewel of Moscow, the most beautiful of all Russia. It has the majesty of past Czars and rulers, and Gorbachev and Yeltsin. The crown jewel has many facets. It has many faces. Maybe the people can learn to reflect its glory through this new way called freedom. There are many changes. There will be many changes. There will be difficulty. Freedom and change take time."

EXCERPTS FROM AN INTERVIEW

Donna Colvis: How long have you resided in the United States?

Bela: For about three years now.

DC: What was happening in Russia before you left?

Bela: Gorbachev had just been dispelled from the party and Yeltsin was appearing on the scene in Parliament. There were ambiguous feelings amongst the people. Some longed for the regiment of Stalin, others were in direct opposition of the Communist party, wanting freedom of speech.

DC: So there are people who still long for Stalin?

Bela: Oh, yes. They admire him like a God. It's Stalin charisma.

DC: How did you feel?

Bela: I personally longed for the freedom that Gorbachev brought about. I think the greatest thing that Gorbachev gave us was the ability to think for ourselves...A freedom of thought and mind.

DC: How did the people react to such a freedom, especially since this was foreign to them?

Bela shares her wonderful smile during her interview.

Bela: That's a good question. There were lots of reactions to this. Some were good and others bad. There was very little organization when the changes came and so we suffered economically. Factories were closed, there was no work for certain people and the lines for food became very long. Those in the political arena were not so competent and viewed their own goals and political ambitions more important than that of the people.

DC: What happened to the Arts during this time?

Bela: Under Stalin, the opera, sports, and most of the Arts were controlled. Now there no longer exists the funding, but, people are able to write and create using their own minds and ideas. All of the controls have been lifted. I think this is much better.

DC: You are from Moscow, what is the condition of Moscow?

Bela: Unfortunately, the face of Moscow has been changed. I believe about three hundred and sixty churches have been destroyed due to various uprisings, but the beauty of the Kremlin remains. Moscow is huge and is composed of many classes of people, from the richest to the poorest. Moscow is dear to me and although some things there have been destroyed, there is a revitalization to restore many of the churches.

DC: What is a favorite tourist spot of Russia?

Bela: Of course, it's Moscow, and the favorite place there is the Kremlin. Tourists are all treated very well and there's so much to see there. You must see the countryside for itself. There exists so much propaganda that one must see things for themselves. For example, we had heard various propaganda about the United States from our newspapers and after being here, I have found a lot not to be true. So, it's important to make your own opinions when you see things for yourself. But I think Moscow is just beautiful! I'm prejudiced because it is my home.

DC: What do you think of the changes in Russia? What of the future?

Bela: I believe all changes are painful, but the growth in Russia will take place for the better. I really think so. I believe it is important to have freedom of speech and freedom to think. I really hope all will go well.

TRY THIS! A TASTE FROM OUR CULTURE...

Borscht (Russia) Borscht

Ingredients:
2 10-oz cans of beets
2 beef/vegetable bouillon cubes mixed with 2C boiling water
2T lemon juice
1C yogurt

Method:
1. Process the beets, bouillon juice and half of the yogurt in a blender or food processor.
2. Cool, then pour into 10 small bowls. Top each serving with a spoonful of the remaining yogurt.

Pickled Eggs

Ingredients:
5 eggs
2C pickled beetroot juice

Method:
1. Boil the eggs for 10 minutes. Cool and shell.
2. Cover the eggs with the beetroot juice and refrigerate them for a week.
3. Remove the eggs and drain well. The eggs are now purple.

A collection of Matroshyka dolls, handmade from Russia.

CHAPTER 7 KOREA

ASIAN PAST

Grandfather sings through windchimes

Ancient bells echo remembrance

Across bellowing seas, far away

Characters 信仅杰, his name

Embodiment of personality.

Sweet incense like smoke signals

Unite past and present, ascend

Wise sage, hair tinted with winter frosts

Gentle voice accompanied by melodies of wind

Missing you...

South Korea

Population 43.1 million

ADOPTIONS

I remember those strange green beans that kept falling from my spoon. I couldn't pick them up and they wouldn't stay on. I wanted my rice and my chopsticks! I was hungry and I just wanted to eat. Frustrated, I began to cry.

I was only three years old when I was adopted and brought to the United States. I never knew of my birth mother or birth father. I only knew of the orphanage where I had been placed in Korea. I do remember the cries of children in the darkness of the night, echoing forever against the bare walls. The cries of children that were never answered. I remember the cold porridge I ate everyday for breakfast until I left for America.

I remember the first day of school when I had turned five. I was so happy because my mother had brought me the most beautiful pink dress with matching bow. I was so excited! In the classroom, there were so many things to play with, a kitchen set and sink, a refrigerator, and even a stove. I started to make friends with the girls who played with me.

Soon I was invited to a friend's house to play. Her name was Carla and she had long yellow pigtails with big bows. My mom drove me to her house.

"Why don't you look like your mom?" Carla asked, "You two look different. You don't have blonde hair."

"I don't know..." I began, "I don't know."

"Where did you get that funny name? It's what? See jing or See jung or Say what?" her older sister teased.

"It is See jung." I answered quietly.

"I have a new bike. Let's play!" said Carla.

And so we played.

Shiori and Miyo sport their native dress.

That episode did not just end there. As I grew older, more and more children made fun of my name and how I looked. Some people called me China doll. Others told me I wasn't American like them and how did my parents have a child that didn't look like them with slanted eyes?

These were the times I cried. I wanted to be like everyone else. I wanted to change my name to Susan to fit in.

My parents were so loving. There was always a supportive hug and kiss with the greatest of understanding. They felt it important to keep my name and culture. They learned how to use chopsticks and they learned how to make Bulgolgi (marinated beef) and rice. Whenever there were Korean festivals in the city nearby, my parents would take me. They tried to teach me as much as they could about my heritage.

After I graduated from college, I spent a year in the place where I had been born, Seoul, Korea as a teacher of English. That experience brought me closer to the language and culture of my people.

Although I've never known my birth parents, I'm happy to be alive. I'm happy to have such loving adoptive parents, and I'm happy to be a Korean American.

Ju Li (See jung's cousin) gives a smile.

Charles stands in front of some Korean decorations

KOREA

EXCERPTS FROM AN INTERVIEW

Donna Clovis: Tell me about your teaching experiences in Korea.

Seejung: It was wonderful and enlightening. I came to Korea speaking only English and had no exposure to the Korean language since I had been adopted. I taught English at one of the American schools in Seoul. Language wasn't a problem there, but I had many more difficulties outside. Finding restaurants, the bathroom, things like that. So I did as any other American tourist, I used my dictionary a lot!

DC: Were there any customs you found difficult to get used to?

Seejung: Oh yes, I couldn't go to the bus without pushing and shoving. It's so crowded in Korea. Koreans don't line up for anything. So they push alot. It's not considered impolite, and even though many women work in Korea, the men always get first preference. They are placed at a higher level than women at work and in the home. That really bothers me because I believe in equality between men and women.

DC: How did this take place? Do you remember any examples?

Seejung: Once at work a woman was up for a promotion as a principal. The directors of the school only gave her a few minutes with the interview and invited all of the men candidates to lunch to discuss the position and additionally interviewed them after. They just didn't give her a chance. That frustrated me because I believed she was a good candidate and just needed to be treated the same as the men.

DC: What is the Korean viewpoint on education? How do they feel about you coming to teach there?

Seejung: Everyone was delightful. They were happy to see me teach and happy I came back to learn more about my culture and language. Education is of primary importance. It is valued amongst the Korean society. The government invests alot of money to educate its children. I believe much more money than the United States.

DC: Was there any turmoil existing in Korea at the time of your stay?

Seejung: Yes. The North Korean people have an atomic bomb. We are not happy about that at all considering how close North Korea is to us. There have been some talks about this between the countries, but things have not gone well. People are really frightened that something may happen.

DC: Was there anything in particular that brought you closer to your culture?

Seejung: Yes, a few things. First, the language. Although I didn't learn to read and write Korean, I did learn to speak it. It made me feel closer to my Korean roots because now I could communicate with the people. When I visited some of the ancient temples and shrines, I was in awe of the beauty and mystery of a culture I really didn't know, but was still very much a part of.

Seejung smiles during her interview.

A Korean display of clothing and articles.

TRY THIS! A TASTE FROM OUR CULTURE...

Bean Curd And Vegetables

Ingredients:
3 cups of fresh or canned green beans, drained
1 cup of shredded carrots
2 tablespoons sesame seeds
1 teaspoon sugar
pinch of salt
1 cake of tofu (you can find tofu in large supermarkets.)

Method:
1. Combine the vegetables together and put them in the refrigerator to cool.
2. Toast the sesame seeds in a frying pan over medium heat, stirring until they are brown. (This will take about two minutes.)
3. Spoon the sesame seeds into a bowl, and let them cool. Crush the seeds between your fingers. Add the sugar and salt to the seeds.
4. Carefully drain the water from the tofu, and place the tofu in a medium-sized bowl. (Tofu is soft and easily falls apart.) Add the sesame seed mixture, and using a spoon, mix the ingredients together.
5. Place the beans and carrots in a serving bowl. Spoon the tofu-sesame mixture over the vegetables. Toss lightly and serve.

CHAPTER 8 SOMALIA

SKELETON SKIN

Skeletons dressed in black, ashy skin

feel desolate desert suns beat upon them

Famine eats away at humanity

Sand dune morgues touch heaven

Parched lips of Somalia beg clouds for rain

and beg belly of Earth for sustenance.

Somalia

Population 6.7 million

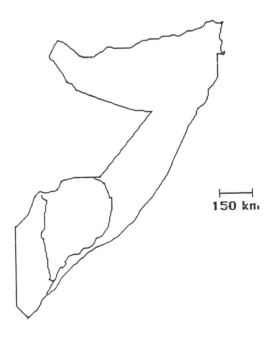

WANDERING

I am a nomad. I have been a nomad all of my life. At the age of sixty, it is not an easy life. The Somali plains are hot and dry. Food is scarce. To protect my dark aging skin, I wear a white toga and a white turban to cover my graying hair. I must continue to move my family from place to place in search of water and pasture for my herds. My family consists of four wives, fourteen children, and two grandparents. My herd is large consisting of several camels, goats, cows, and sheep.

We are thirsty now and our lips are parched from the heat. We long for a watering hole or well. The camels are burdened down with our beehive huts and cooking utensils. They are in need of water too. I hope we find a good place for pasture soon.

In the distance, we can see a crowded place. People hovering over one spot. And green, grassy plain lying beyond them. We step up our pace, hoping that this will be the fertile spot to set up camp. And surely it is - a well and the people hovering around are sharing tales and stories about the cities far away. There is plenty of water. You can see from their faces that they are happy. We gather water from the well for my family. Then we gather water for the herds. As my family sets up camp upon fertile ground nearby, I begin to engage in talk about the goings on in Mogadishu, a place I have only visited once in my life.

And the older men tell me that there are many goings on in Mogadishu. Food is becoming scarce due to the warlords hoarding. Famine is spreading quickly through Somalia. People are beginning to die. The numbers are becoming too many to count. An older man has lost two wives and two children already. We are told that we

An African woman shows a hand painted mask.

must go into the cities for food when we run out of good fertile ground. We pray that the earth will birth itself with plenty. There is more and more violence in the cities. Death is a plague to our land. How long for the time of our forefathers. A time of peace and plenty. We express how grateful we all are to have a life in the wilderness, but we fear that soon we will be suffering also. Although life as a nomad is hard and difficult, it is not a way for violence, like the violence taking place in Mogadishu.

Perhaps we will talk more about our solutions for peace after we set up our houses. Perhaps we can drink our hot spice tea around the fire and exchange tales of hope and songs of the past. Perhaps our people will find a solution. I pray. I hope.

EXCERPTS FROM AN INTERVIEW

Donna Clovis: Omar, what type of job did you have in Somalia?

Omar: I was a doctor in a hospital in Mogadishu.

DC: How did the famine and crossfire affect you?

Omar: Oh, in many, many ways. Our hospital was already over-crowded and with poor facilities. With the increase of troops and famine, more and more people were brought in. We had no air conditioning and many times we were without medicines. We had those wounded by the war and others starving from the famine. I was tired and sad because I couldn't help more people. Many times, I was too exhausted to help others. More and more babies and children were dying from starvation, and we had very little if any food to give them. There was a feeding station set up by the UN nearby with rice given to people twice a day. There was hot, sweltering heat and flies. One could smell death everywhere.

DC: How did all of this come to affect Somalia?

Omar: Our government had been ruled for nearly twenty-one years by Mohammed Siad Barre. Then the government was toppled and we've had anarchy, no law or government in Somalia since. That all began in January of 1991. There has been fighting amongst different groups and clans of people. Of course, with the desert heat in Somalia, famine is common, but it has been worsened because certain warlords are hoarding the food and the food is not getting to the people.

DC: Did the feeding stations set up by the UN help feed the people?

Omar: Yes, somewhat. But as you know with the hoarding and the great famine, nothing was enough. Twice a day people were fed rice and beans cooked in large pans over fire. It was at least something to sustain life.

DC: How did the Somali people feel about the troops in Somalia?

Omar: Some were happy. Others just wanted to survive and didn't care. Others were suspicious, they did not want foreigners in their land. Some people thought America might take over. Some Somali people wanted to solve their own problems and didn't want any inter-ference from the other countries. That's when more of the violence began, between the warlords, the different clans, and those afraid of the loss of their own government. There were many people who took advantage of the situation by becoming bandits and robbers. It was certainly confusing and bloody.

DC: Weren't the Somali people told that the duty of the UN troops was to allow for the protection of food for the people?

Omar: Sure, but there were people who were frightened by the guns and troops and felt that they would loose control of their govern-ment. That feeling spread throughout the countryside rapidly, and I believe that the UN troops were after Aidid. There were so many different stories going on. I had also heard that the UN was trying to help Somalia establish their government, but the Somali people felt they could do it on their own without outside interference.

DC: Were Somalis happy with the gradual removal of troops from their country.

Omar: Again, feelings were mixed. Some were happy. Others were afraid. And even others did not want them to leave. But I would say the majority of Somali's people felt that eventually they could solve their own problems. Over 300,000 people have died because of the fighting and famine, maybe now better things can happen.

DC: Do you think Somalis will be able to solve their problems?

Omar: All countries have many problems. All we can do is hope that all nations will be able to solve their own problems. I don't know. I have much apathy. We hope and we pray.

TRY THIS! A TASTE FROM OUR CULTURE...

Baked Yam Chips (Africa)

Ingredients:
1 lb yam
salt to taste

Method:
1. Peel the yam, then slice it into paper-thin slices.
2. Arrange the slices on an oiled cookie sheet and sprinkle with salt.
3. Bake in a hot oven (400° F) until crispy.

CHAPTER 9 GERMANY

BERLIN

Blood-stained thumbprints

etched upon the wall, invisible

its frizzy barbed wire hair, tightly curled from rains of past

stand in remembrance of grandmother

who attempted to by-pass its brick heart

feel her dying pulse

I leave footprints weeping, melting in snow

walking pass to the other side.

Germany

Population 79.5 million

100 km

THE WALL

Ahhh...The beauty of Germany. From the dense green forests of mountains to the deep valley gorges of the Rhine. In winter, snow masks the countrysides and with the birth of spring, greenery rises in the warmth of the sun. Smell the crisp, clean air of the mountains. As you near my small, quaint cottage, you will entertain other smells. Yes, the smells of my Abendbrot (open face sandwiches) and home-made soups. Cooking is my craft, my hobby. All of my foods are homemade and made perfect by my eighty-six years of practice. Come and visit any evening and sample dumplings and sausage and noodles or sauces. Enough to fill your belly and more.

With the beauty and fill of this wonderful place, there are memories, very sad and old memories about The Wall. That eerie, crumbling and dark barbed-wire remembrance of lost family and friends.

Thousands of people had left East Germany before the Wall was built, in the old times. Dad and I were among the ones who had left. Mother would come later because Grandmother was ill and could not make the trip as yet. Mother was supposed to nurse her to health before they came. It was supposed to take several weeks. That's all.

So we waited on the other side, and began preparing a new way of life. Dad got an apartment for us, and we would wait for mother and grandmother to come, but they never did. We lost contact with them. We didn't know what had happened. We didn't know if grandmother had died or was very sick. But we did know that the Wall was being built and people were no longer being allowed to come over to the other side. We feared the worse, that mother and grandmother tried to crossover, but perhaps were shot. Many were killed trying to escape the Wall. When the western borders were fortified, we knew

Olga shows her native dress.

that was the end of all hope. It was as if mother and grandmother were sealed within an eternal grave or tomb, never to be seen again. But the worse was not knowing. The emptiness still rests within my heart after all of these years.

Now with the Wall down, I long to find out exactly what happened, but that is not easy. For I am eighty-six now and I have a hard time getting around these days. All records are not available and the graves of those killed remain unmarked. I must look to the future. The future of my generations. I have three lovely daughters and six lovely grandchildren. I am happy that we all are free. I hope families will never again suffer the hatred and pain brought about by the Wall.

EXCERPTS FROM AN INTERVIEW

Donna Clovis: How did you come to be in the United States?

Andri: I came here to visit some of my family.

DC: How did you feel when the Great Wall was removed between East and West Germany?

Andri: Of course, at first I was very happy. Very happy that the democracy could spread to another part of Europe that was hidden by Communism. The tearing down of the wall has meant other things for us in West Germany.

DC: What has it meant?

Andri: Because the economy was so low in East Germany, there was a large number of East Germans coming into West Germany looking for jobs. Then the government was trying to make both sides, East and West Germany equal. Many West Germans have lost their jobs, like me. I used to work in the steel mill and I had other friends that worked in the coal mines. Thousands of people have lost their jobs. As it is, Germany must compete with other countries in the goods they produce and technology and computers. We were having a hard time doing that before the wall was removed.

DC: Tell me about the attacks on foreigners in Germany?

Andri: I don't want you to think that Germans are such wild people that we attack foreigners. That is just not true. But there have been attack on certain immigrant people who want to live in Germany because of the economy. We Germans do not have jobs. Why should we allow foreign people to come and take our jobs away from us? People get very angry about this because they want to survive. They don't do it because people are just foreigners, if you understand what I mean. But we must eat and feed our families. Germany belongs first to Germans. You understand that uniting East and West Germany did not bring all good and riches. We are happy and very sad at the same time.

DC: Do the attacks against these immigrants continue?

Andri: Not anymore because the government does not allow many immigrants to stay in Germany so that the economy can get better. The attacks are now very few and very low.

DC: What solutions have the Germans come up with to deal with such problems?

Andri: Many companies went to a four day work week. Others have taken many, many cuts in their paycheck. And still many people have lost their jobs. I don't think any of these things are helping the government or the people.

DC: How did you lose your job at the steel mill?

Andri: I worked there for many, many years. But now you can get steel for very cheap prices from the East. They don't need any of the high paid workers from the West anymore. It's terrible. Everyone is afraid. Afraid of losing their jobs and afraid they cannot eat and feed their families.

DC: So do you think the removal of the Wall is a good thing or a bad thing?

Andri: That's a hard question. Sometimes good changes bring with them bad changes. We must go through this in order to become a Democracy. Things take time. But I don't have much patience and neither do many people when you try to live from day to day.

TRY THIS! A TASTE FROM OUR CULTURE...

St. Lucia Buns

Ingredients:
1 Package sweetmilk buscuit dough
20 Currants
1/2 C icing sugar
2 t Cream

Method:
1. Divide the package into 10 biscuits.
2. Roll each biscut into a 10-in. strip of dough. Curl the strip into an S-shape, then curl each end into a spiral. Put a currant in the middle of each spiral. The currants symbolize St. Lucia's watchful eyes.
3. Cook the biscuts as directed.
4. While the biscuits are still warm, brush the tops with icing made with the icing sugar and cream.

Bob and Maria sport smiles

Andri gives his mother a hug.

CHAPTER 10 INDIA

BOMBAY IN MY HEART

Although I speak many languages

I dream in one

School teachers say, Speak English!

Mother says, Wear your sari!

Speak your native tongue!

I have one voice

One human spirit

One Dream...

India

Population 866.4 million

500 km

I DON'T SPEAK ENGLISH

My name is Udayan. I came from India last week. I am ten years old. Today is my first day of school. I'm afraid because it is a new school and I don't understand English. My own language is Hindu. It is one of the many languages of India. My mother and father speaks it. So does my auntie and uncle. We have come to the United States to live with them until we have enough money for our own house. Auntie and uncle have been here for four years. They speak English very well.

Auntie and uncle and mother take me to the school. Mother tells me that they will take good care of me here and she will come back for me at the end of the day. Auntie and uncle and mother kiss me good-bye. I don't want them to leave me. They are the only ones who understand what I say and how I feel.

A tall lady with yellow hair grabs my hand and takes me to a classroom. The classroom looks very different from the small school-house I used to go to in India. There are many new things I have never seen before. There are many boys and girls sitting at their desks, and they look very different from my friends in India. Some have red and yellow hair. Others are very white. And yet others are very black. Only two have the brown color of my skin. We had two large tables in our schoolhouse where we used to study. The warm air and the hot sun used to shine through the windows.

The lady tells the teacher my name. That's the only word I understand. The teacher places a desk next to her where I sit. She takes out a book and reads it to the class. I listen, but I don't understand.

The teacher speaks again and the children stand up. They take their lunch bags and boxes from their desks. I guess I must do this

A woman from India displays her musical instrument.

too. Mother made my favorite lunch today from my country. It's roti and vegetables. It is very spicy. I like spicy food. I take my lunch from my desk too.

The children line up at the door. The teacher takes me by the hand and places me in line with the others. A girl behind me touches me and speaks. I don't understand , so I say nothing. She touches me again, but this time she is laughing. She is laughing and pointing at my clothes. I don't understand what she is saying, but I know she is being mean.

My clothes are different from the other children. They are my cotton green shorts and cotton shirt from India. They are very special because my Grandma made them for me. I miss Grandma and Grandpa. They used to live with us in our house in India. I miss my cousins and I miss my friends.

I begin to cry. The teacher comes to me and holds my hands. She whispers some words I do not understand. She takes me to the front of the line with her. We walk to the lunchroom. The children sit down and eat.

The teacher takes me to a different table with other children. She places me next to a girl. She looks like me and as the teacher says her name, I know she is from my country, India. The girl says hi to me in my language, Namaste! I smile and say Namaste too.

I'm so happy to have a friend that understands me. As we eat, we talk in my language. I'm very happy now. My new friend tells me about two American children who are very nice friends. She brings them to me after lunch on the playground. I don't understand what they say, but my friend tells me in my language. They want to be my friend too and they want to help me learn English.

I'm happy to have friends. Maybe I will like school here. Maybe I will like America.

EXCERPTS FROM AN INTERVIEW

Donna Clovis: When you think of your country India, what comes to your mind?

Amartya: Diversity. India is diversity. There are so many different languages. I believe there are about three hundred different languages in India alone. There are different cultures in India and they vary depending upon where you live. There are different rituals and festivals and they differ depending on the region. There are strong and varying opinions about religion and linguistics and culture.

DC: What are the official languages of India?

Amartya: They are Hindu and English, but there are at least fourteen other languages that are official. Some of them are Bengali, Urdu, Punjabi, and Sanskrit.

DC: What else is special about India?

Amartya: I believe the extended family is special. This is not so common in the United States. It is normal for us to live with our parents, grandparents, aunts, and uncles. The family unit is very important to us in India. The family is more important than the person himself. We feel it is important to take care of our older ones.

DC: What type of government exists in India?

Amartya: It is a democracy. It is a well established democracy. It is true that the government is no longer ruled by anyone of the Nehru family and that caused a little bit of upheaval, but we have a good democracy. It is stable. Since 1991, we have an open economy. You must understand, we have great pride in who we are as Indians and yet, we find excuses for what is bad. I guess all people are like that. We have a superiority and inferiority complex. All people are like that.

DC: How does India feel about the complexities of the world it competes with?

Amartya: The world is certainly complex and Indian society realizes especially now, the importance of keeping up with the world and is making every effort to do this through education.

DC: What are your favorite foods?

Amartya: I love rice and vegetables, and lentil with meat and curry. It is quite good.

DC: And your favorite festival?

Amartya: I'am Hindu and for most Hindus Diwali is the most important holiday. It is the Indian festival of lights. We celebrate an ancient story about the return of Prince Ram to his people, and we welcome him with many lights. I also like Dushera which comes before and leads up to Diwali.

An Indian family smiles during their interview.

DC: What part of India are you from and is this festival popular in that region?

Amartya: I am from Bihar and it is the capital of one of India's states. My wife is from Bombay, and Diwali is one of the most popular celebrations.

DC: How long will you stay in the United States?

Amartya: Both of us are students at the University. We plan to go back to India for six months and we will return to finish our studies in the United States.

DC: Will you seek permanent residency here?

Amartya: We love the United States, but most of our family is still in India and we shall return to them.

TRY THIS! A TASTE FROM OUR CULTURE...

Rotis

Ingredients:
2 C rice flour
1/2 C unsweetened shredded coconut
1 t salt
1 C water
2 t oil

Method:
1. Mix the first 4 ingredients together. Form into 10 balls, then flatten.
2. Fry on a greased griddle. Turn once to brown on both sides.

Barfi Balls (East Indian)

Ingredients:
1/2 C butter
3/4 C sugar
3/4 C milk
2 C powered milk
1 C ground almonds
1/4 C unsweetened shredded coconut

Method:
1. Melt the butter in a large saucepan over low heat.
2. Stir in sugar and the liquid milk. Bring to a boil and boil hard for 5 minutes.
3. Remove from the heat and add the powdered milk. Stir in the almonds and coconut.
4. When cool, form into balls.

CHAPTER 11 NATIVE HAWAIIANS

SYMPHONY IN E MINOR

The dischord of the world is loud

but take the time to see

the music of a faint but proud

classical symphony.

Hear cymbals of the ocean waves

which beat against the shore

here lutes of graceful seagull slaves

their solos to adore.

And if someone should tell me,

a God does not exist

because man's world is out of key

and problems do persist.

Just take a walk along the sands...

Just listen to Nature's concert bands...

United States of America

Population 252.5 million

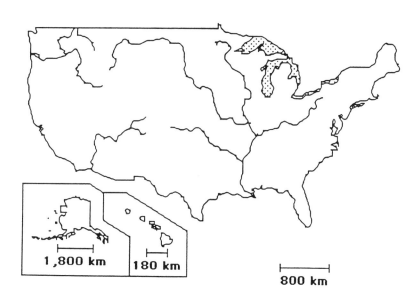

PARADISE

Tourists had camped out all night in the "House of the Sun" to see it. We had climbed a steep crater in the middle of the night in the state park to be prepared to view it. Soon faint beams of light from the dawn stretched beyond the rim of this dark volcanic crater. Inch by inch the sun appeared in the dark blue Hawaiian sky. We had witnessed the amazing rising of the sun from this vantage point. A glorious sight indeed.

Here in this state park we are able to take a glimpse of paradise. The lush green valleys and lava deserts paint the landscapes. Black sand beaches of the Big Island embrace the smells of fresh guava, coconut, and papaya fruits. Waterfalls decorate the peaks of Mauna Kea and banana plants engulf all forms of tropical life.

The diversity of beauty does not end here! Consider the mosaic of peoples who inhabit the Hawaiian islands. They are Chinese, Japanese, Korean, African American, Hawaiian, Caucasian, Samoan, Latino, and Phillipino. It is indeed the "Meeting place of the East and West." Diversity can be found in the various ethnic foods and festivals and architecture. Diversity can be found in the sounds of the languages echoing in the past and present. The ethnic richness is found in the making of the "leis" of fragrant orchid fruit or flowers. It is found in the decorative cloaks made of many bird feathers. It is found in sculpture and dances like the "Hula."

Tourism has meant survival and revenue for the islands of Hawaii. Will tourism result in a paradise lost or a paradise maintained? What of Hawaii's future? With more tourism, comes the building of more hotels and roads. Then the cutting down of more forests and jungles, and the displacement of Native peoples and their way of life as well as the various species of animals hidden within the foliage. Will Hawaii remember the Native peoples way to be good to the land or nature? Or will Native peoples be made extinct through the revenues of tourism? Will Hawaii's anthem continue to ring with truth through the centuries:

Hawaii's own

Look to our king

The royal chief

The chief.

Chorus:

Royal father

Kamehameha

We shall defend

With spears.

Hawaii's own

Look to your chiefs

The children after you

The young

Hawaii's own

O nation

Your great duty

Strive.

EXCERPTS FROM AN INTERVIEW

Donna Clovis: Hawaii is such a beautiful paradise. What do you like most about it?

Neil: I love the ocean. As a child that was my favorite place to be.

Dee: I love the waterfalls. That's my favorite place to be when I want peace. It is so tranquil!

DC: And yet with the beauty I hear that there are threats of extinction.

Dee: Yes, not just of animals, but of Native people like us.

Neil: There was a time when this paradise was all ours. We are struggling to hold on to our culture and our lands.

DC: To begin, what do you do for a living here in Hawaii?

Neil: We both clean rooms at one of the hotels in Waikiki.

DC: Where do you live?

Dee: We live in Papkolea. It is a homestead for Native Hawaiians.

DC: Is that similar to a reservation?

Dee: Yes, it is.

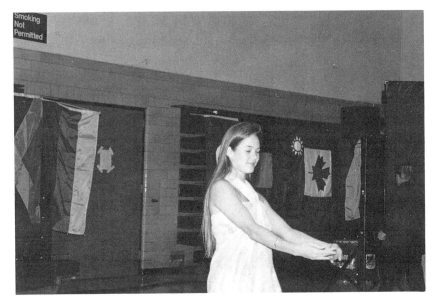

Candy, a native Hawaiian, demonstrates the Hula.

DC: What is life like on the homestead?

Neil: First of all, the homestead is for people of at least 50% Hawaiian blood. That was determined by the government. It is a silly law. How can you tell how much Hawaiian blood a person has. Our culture prides itself on oral tradition of ancestry, but the government won't listen to that.

Dee: We sleep in a tent. We have two small children. The conditions are very poor. I must cook using a small gas stove. It's terrible. We've lost our land and our culture. Now we must live like this!

DC: Can you still preserve your language?

Dee: That's difficult. When settlers came here we were told not to speak Hawaiian, so therefore, we have lost our language too.

DC: What do you think the solution is?

Neil: Native Hawaiians should be given a voice in the government. We should have some control, after all, we were here first. But now, everything is so commercial. Everyone wants power and money.

Dee: People can be fooled when they think of Hawaii. Many people think of paradise. My people think of it with great sadness and a loss of hope.

DC: Many cultures do manage to keep their traditions alive. What do you think you can do?

Dee: Speak our language in our homes and keep the native foods and dances.

DC: What hope is there economically?

Neil: Maybe if we work hard we can buy a small apartment so we don't have to live in tents outside. We need to move away from this homestead.

Dee: We will. We are determined to make a better life for our kids.

DC: What advice do you give to your kids?

Neil: Be proud of who you are and keep your culture.

TRY THIS! A TASTE FROM OUR CULTURE...

Coconut Chips (Hawaiian)

Ingredients:
1 coconut
salt and sugar to taste

Method:
1. Cut open the coconut and scoop out the pulp. Use a vegetable peeler to slice the pulp thinly into strips.
2. Toast the strips in the oven at 400° F for 5 minutes or until brown and crisp. Sprinkle half with salt and half with sugar.

CHAPTER 12 ISRAEL

SIRENS

She combs coarse strands, doll's hair

Imagining, cuddling innocence

White angry sparks, fireworks of war

lunge forth against black silhouette skies.

Roaring planes, sirens sing lullabies

Broken boughs and branches

shell and mortar fall around

a baby with dreams.

Israel

Population 4.5 million

50 km

SEARCHING FOR PEACE AND FREEDOM

Tonight is a special evening. We shall celebrate freedom. We shall celebrate freedom for Jews all over the world. It is the night of Passover (Pesach). We shall read from the Haggadah, the book that tells the Passover story. We shall learn the importance of the matzo or unleavened bread, and the maror (bitter herbs), and roasted lamb. The haroset is important too because it symbolizes the mortar used by the Jews to build the cities of Egypt. Haroset is a mixture of nuts, apples, and wine. We will also learn about the symbolism behind karpas (like parsley) and the egg and wine. All of these foods are important to the Seder, our feast. We shall remember and we shall celebrate the time when Moses led the Jews out of Egypt from bondage and slavery. We shall celebrate freedom!

As we begin the Seder, we hear the gunfire outside. With each piercing shot, we cringe. You would think we would be used to the sounds of warfare by now, but we are not. It is not a normal sound. It is not a happy sound. We are constantly reminded of death and the unfriendly noise of war. We long and pray for peace.

Our land is Israel, the Holy Land. It is a beautiful place with fertile valleys and lands overlooking the Mediterranean Sea. It is a place of infinite history. From the hills you can get a glimpse of the magnificence of Jerusalem and other cities with their domed roofs and streets bustling with people.

As we finish our Passover celebration we continue to hear the gunfire in the background. How we long for peace in this part of the world.

Shalom.

EXCERPTS FROM AN INTERVIEW

Donna Clovis: What is the most interesting thing about Israel?

Avi: There are so many interesting things. That is a very difficult question. First, I think that the fact that Jews come from all over the world to live here. I think that is amazing. I do not think there is another place like Israel on the face of the Earth. There are also so many different types of Jews. Some are light and some are dark. Some have straight hair and others curly hair. Some are blonde and others have black hair. There are Sephardic Jews from the Middle East and North Africa, and Ashkenic Jews from Europe, specifically from Germany and Russia. We are such a diverse people, but united in Judaism. I think many American people do not know what diversity there is amongst the Jews.

DC: Some people mistake what the word "Jewish" means. What does it mean to you?

Avi: A Jew is Jewish by nationality and religion, but, in Israel, a person can have three different identities. I know that seems confusing, but there is citizenship, religion, and nationality. I give you this example. A person can be an Israeli by citizenship and a christian by religion or a person can be an Arab by nationality and Israeli by citizenship all at the same time. Confusing isn't it?

DC: Then what languages are spoken in Israel?

Avi: Hebrew and Arabic are the official languages. English is also

Mia from Israel stands in front of a mural painted by her daughter.

used and because so many come from other countries, there are many other languages like German and Russian and some African dialects that are spoken in the homes of many Jews. That too, is not an easy question to answer.

DC: Describe the neighborhood that you live in.

Avi: Ahh, it is so different than in America. In America, people do not take the time to get to know each other. They really do not look at each other and say hello. That was very difficult for me when I first came to visit this country. I am very friendly and my neighborhood was very friendly. Everyone knows each other and everyone knows each family. There is a sense of a close community. We know each other's names and I can say that that is so different in America. Do you know the names of your neighbors? Not only do we know all the names, but we can tell you about each person in the family. We love company and we love them to visit our homes to eat and talk. We love new friends too and we love to hear what they have to say.

DC: What are your favorite foods?

Avi: I love all foods! But my favorite food is Falafel.

DC: Describe Falafel.

Avi: It is a type of pita bread with chick peas that are fried. It is a wonderful national treat. You should try it.

DC: What is your favorite holiday?

Avi: Pesach or Passover. It means so much to me because it means freedom for all Jews. Freedom is so important to Jews and all people. And this is the time where all the family will come together. Family is so important.

DC: And the issue of freedom reminds me of the issues of peace. Do you think peace will be attained in the Middle East?

Avi: That is my prayer. Our prayer is that our homeland will soon be free of war, violence, pain and hurt. We have suffered so much. We do not need to suffer anymore. That is our hope and that is our prayer.

TRY THIS! A TASTE FROM OUR CULTURE...

Charoset (Jewish)

Charoset is eaten at the Seder meal as a symbol of the mortar used by the Jewish slaves who built pyramids for the Egyptian pharaoh. It is usually made with red wine, but grape juice can be substituted.

Ingredients:
1 apple
1/3 C chopped walnuts
1/4 t cinnamon
2 T grape juice

Method:
1. Peel and chop the apple.
2. Add the nuts, cinnamon, and grape juice. Mix well.

Matzot meal chremslach (Jewish)

Ingredients:
1 egg, separated
1/4 C water
1/4 C matzot meal
dash of salt and pepper
1 T vegetable oil

Method:
1. Beat the egg white until stiff.
2. Combine the yoke, water, meal, salt and pepper. Fold in the egg white.
3. Grease a griddle with the oil. Drop the matzot mixture by table-spoons onto the griddle and brown on both sides.

CHAPTER 13 CHINA

TIANANMEN SQUARE

Great wall, ancient fortress encircles dynasties of the past

Students smolder,

smoke of discontent ascends, signals westward

Beijing

Tanks trample freedoms, metal grinds flesh

Blood perspires through crumbling cement,

Great Wall

Outcries touch the moon

Milky moon drips tears.

China

Population 1.151 billion

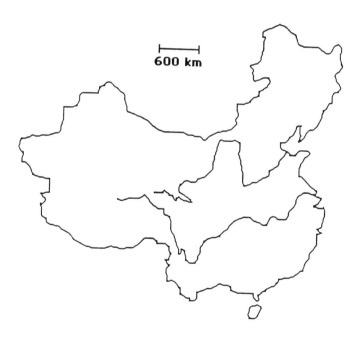

TIANAMEN SQUARE

I tried to warn the students who were protesting in Tianamen Square. I lived only a few blocks away from the demonstrations and found myself bringing water to those students who were now fasting. They were getting weaker and weaker and the Square was getting more crowded and dirty. Students from all over China kept coming, and Tianamen Square began to smell because of the waste. We all wanted freedom, but I knew the government would not change overnight and this was not the way to change the government. The protest had gone too far. I was sick with fear and remorse with the possibility of what could happen. So my neighbors and I went to the students again and begged them to leave. We begged them to leave because we were older and wiser and knew that the protest could lead to the needless death of many young people. We had spent many years under the Communist regime and knew there were other ways to negotiate and get the attention of the government.

I knew my wrinkled skin and grey hair was a symbol to the students of the old way of life under Communism, but my heart yearned for freedom too. How I wanted to express my ideas and thoughts! How I wanted to be free from censorships! How I wanted to experience freedom before my death! We explained there was a better way, but no one listened. It was as if my feeble voice had faded into the gentle wind blowing through the stench of the Square. We knew the government was soon to intervene. How could they continue to ignore the confusion in the Square?

And as we had thought these words and uttered them from the depth of our souls, it occurred. Tanks rolled their way through the Square telling all to leave or else be killed. As we feared, the

The Yen family from China.

students ignored the warning. They continued to cry for freedom. The tanks began firing upon the crowds. There were some of my older neighbor friends who died too because they ran in front of the tanks trying to stop the government. They tried to tell the tanks that the students were too young and too stupid and did not know what they were doing. They wanted another day to permit the students to leave, but the mighty government did not hear their cries and screams above the loudness and roars of the tanks as they plowed through the streets and neighborhoods into the Square.

Many were killed. I lost a very good elderly friend in Tianamen Square. She wanted to save the lives of youth. She would rather die than have one young person perish. I pass her house daily and remember the echoes of her hello.

The cries and screams haunt me in my sleep to this day. I don't sleep very well since then. The sun continues to rise and set upon mainland China. Not much has changed here since Tianamen Square.

EXCERPTS FROM AN INTERVIEW

Donna Clovis: What comes to mind when you think of Tianamen Square in China?

Jian-yu: I think of my rights for freedom and the many students who participated in the student movement there.

DC: How did you participate in the student movement?

Jian-yu: There were many demonstrations for freedom of speech and freedom of the press for democracy. All newspapers and television programs are controlled by the government and the people cannot say their opinions.

DC: How restricted were your freedoms of the press and speech?

Jian-yu: They were completely restricted. If a Communist leader did something bad, it would not be reported. If a person wrote something in the newspaper that the government did not like, it would be deleted before the newspaper was printed. There was no place for the people to talk and give input into the way the government was run.

DC: What caused the violence and the many deaths in Tianamen Square?

Jian-yu: There were many demonstrations which took place here over a period of time, from April to June 1989. Then the students had a hunger strike and refused to eat. The slogan became Freedom or

Death! Students from all over China came and crowded Tianamen Square. At first, the government did not respond, but when Tianamen Square became so disorderly, they began to react. I remember that there were some of us who tried to persuade the students to go home because there might be big trouble from the government.

DC: I thought you wanted Freedom of Press and Speech, why would you encourage the students to leave?

Jian-Yu: We wanted peaceful demonstration. Things were too large and disorderly at this time. I believe it is impossible to ask for so much from the Communist government at one time. Changes come with time, not all at once. The hunger strike was now going on for two weeks. Many people, including myself sought donations of drink to help the students.

DC: What did the government finally do?

Jian-Yu: The government then issued a law to protect and control Tianamen Square. I would say Tianamen Square was about ten times the size of an average elementary school and it was extremely crowded. The army was placed on the outskirts of the entire Square. Then two tanks proceeded into the Square shooting. People tried to escape and yet others fought back with homemade bombs. Everyone was ordered to leave the Square by 4:00 A.M. in the morning. If they didn't leave, they would be shot. Many people tried to protect the students from the gunfire and they were killed.

DC: Do you know how many were killed?

Jian-Yu: Some say Two hundred and others say three hundred. But I was there and I believe there were many more killed than reported.

DC: What happened then?

Jian-Yu smiles during his interview.

Jian-Yu: The government cleaned the bodies and debris from the Square and remained in the Square for some time. They also tried to arrest the leaders of the movement in order to silence them.

DC: Do you think the movement accomplished anything?

Jian-Yu: Not right away, but after one year, people were able to give input and criticism to the government. Things got worse after Tianamen Square for awhile, because the government was so protective, but like I said, after a year, they began to listen. It is remarkable that the government can actually now hear and take criticism from its people. Change will take place in China slowly and lots of things will aid in the change like economic conditions and social movements.

DC: What else is Tianamen Square known for?

Jian-Yu: It is a very famous place. It was part of an ancient emperor's forbidden city. Now it is famous for freedom.

DC: Why have you come to the United States?

Jian-Yu: I am studying here. I will be here for three years and then return to Beijing.

DC: Thanks, I wish you the best. That was an exciting story!

TRY THIS! A TASTE FROM OUR CULTURE...

Egg Drop Soup (Chinese)

Ingredients:
5 chicken bouillon cubes
5 C boiling water
1 beaten egg (from blown-out egg)
chopped chives or parsley or radish sprouts

Method:
1. Boil the water with the cubes until the cubes dissolve.
2. Whisk the beaten egg into the mixture.
3. Take off the heat and serve immediately, topped with chives.

CHAPTER 14 AFRICAN AMERICANS

ENCORE!

Musical notes

flash as lightning

in crowded ghetto sky

Feel wetness of rhythm

Staccato rain on charcoal streets,

Rap of feathered pen

and pirouetting feet.

Euphonic chorus of Arts

thunders forth center stage

A theatrical performance

well done.

Applaud the vibrance of the color brown!

United States of America

Population 252.5 million

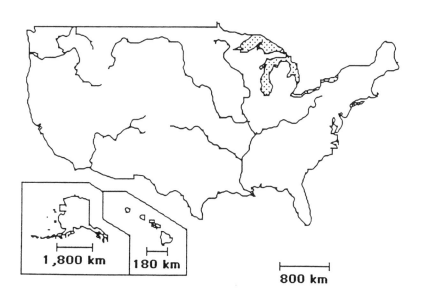

HARAMBEE!

Habari gani! It is a Swahili greeting for Welcome or What's the news? Welcome to our Kwanzaa festivities. It is the seventh evening of Kwanzaa and all of our relatives have come to our Karamu celebration. The inside of our house is decorated with small white lights and evergreens. They are draped across the doorways and banisters of the stairs. Mom has decorated the house with beauty and the house smells of African foods. We will light the Kinara which holds seven candles. We will remember each of the seven principles of Kwanzaa. Grandad tells us how important these principles are in the lives of African Americans.

"Umoja means unity," Grandad begins, "We must strive to be harmonious as a family, nation, and African American community. Who knows the second principle?"

"I do." I said waving my hands frantically.

"Jason, what do you think?"

"It is Ku ku. It means self-determination."

"You mean Kujichagulia. That's a hard one for a small guy like you to pronounce," Grandad chuckled, "It means that we define ourselves, create for ourselves, and speak for ourselves instead of letting others do it for us. What about the third principle?" Grandad looked about for a hand amongst all of the aunts and uncles and cousins seated before him.

"I know" little cousin Anna said, "It is ujima."

"And Ujima means collective work and responsibilities. It means we must build our own businesses and control the economics of our communities, sharing the wealth." Grandad added.

"I know the next one," Grandma chimed in, "It's Ujamaa.

Mary smiles during the family's African American celebration.

That's the one I always remember. It means to build our own shops and stores and profit together."

"Anyone remember the fifth principle?" Grandad asked curiously.

"Nia!" my sister Melissa yelled.

"Nia means purpose" I added.

"That means we will restore our people to their traditional greatness." Grandad explained, And the sixth principle?"

"Kuumba," Dad started, "It means creativity. We must do everything we can to make our community beautiful."

"The last one is Imani. Imani means faith," Auntie said, "We must always believe with our whole heart in our creator, our parents, and our leaders, and that we will have victory after our struggle."

"Now," Grandad said in a low and gruff voice, "Now the toast."

I jumped up with joy because this is my favorite part of Kwaanza. It is my sister's favorite part too. We love saying the seven Harambees. It means let's pull together, but first we all remember our ancestors or relatives. We mention each one by name and why they are important to us today. All of them have given us life and many good things. They have given us courage.

Now it's time for the Harambees. Harambee! Harambee! We say this seven times with great excitement. After the Harambees, it's time to eat all of the wonderful African foods Mom has prepared. There's fried chicken, turkey and pecan pie. I think this is the part that Dad loves the best. He loves to eat.

I love this feast. I love my family. I love being an African American. Harambee!

EXCERPTS FROM AN INTERVIEW

Donna Clovis: Tell us a little about yourself?

Dr. Williams: I am retired now. I have a doctoral degree in Business Administration. I now participate in projects to help the homeless and other less fortunate people.

DC: What does it mean to be African American?

Dr. Williams: It is a heritage I am proud of. It is a heritage of struggle and then it is a heritage of triumph.

DC: How is it a heritage of struggle and then how is it a heritage of triumph?

Dr. Williams: I must think about that question. It is not an easy question to answer. It is a heritage of struggle because we have not yet achieved equality. Yes, we have made great strides since slavery, but we are not free. The opportunities presented us are not the same. Many times, we must be better than the next person to get the same job. We must have more degrees or graduate with the highest of honors. We continue to struggle against the glass ceilings in corporations. We are not yet part of the political systems which operate in the workplace. We struggle with Black on Black crime. Yes, our lives are not struggle free, and yet, we are a heritage of triumph. Consider the many middle-class African Americans with good educations and homes, with beautiful, educated children who aspire to have the very best that life has to offer. The wonderful inventions and literature created by African Americans. The media does not give enough good coverage of what is positive amongst African Americans. The media tends to focus on the bad, giving bad impressions about African Americans. We have triumphed over slavery, but we still have a ways to go.

DC: What impact does the media have on coverage of African Americans?

Dr. Williams: The media could have a good impact, however, it constantly reports on all the wrongs of African Americans. It can provide very negative stereotypes that promote prejudice.

DC: What would you like the media to cover?

Dr. Williams: The accomplishments of African Americans, young and old, rich and poor. There needs to be more attention on those who are successful. We need more positive role models in the media. We need to show that African Americans can be doctors and lawyers, teachers and principals, not just athletes and singers. Our children as well as children of all races need to see African Americans in different roles of success.

DC: What advice would you give young people?

Dr. Williams: To be the best that you can. Never give up. Never allow racism to be an excuse for not doing well in life.

DC: What celebrations do you hold dear?

Dr. Williams: I love Kwanzaa. I love it because it is meant to unite families and remember ancestors and relatives. I feel that there is not enough attention placed upon the family unit in our country and for that reason, children do not have the support systems they need to be successful. I love my family. To me, the family means life.

DC: What of the future? What do you think will help unite America?

Dr. Williams: I believe we must first confront our racism. Then all races must communicate to come up with solutions. We are all dependent upon each other. I feel our society has forgotten the important lessons and words of Dr. Martin luther King. During the sixties there was more unity between Blacks and whites. Both participated in the marches for freedom. We must unite again just like that. We must learn to love and cease to hate. We must realize that the future of America rests upon all races becoming united. It is not an easy solution. We must continue to talk and work to find solutions to our problems.

DC: Do you believe this will happen?

Dr. Williams: I pray every day that it happens. There are communities throughout the United States who are making this happen. Some people realize that we all want good things, the same things for our children. What future will there be for America if it doesn't? It must happen. Everyone must take their share and make it happen. I know that it is not an easy task, but for our survival as a nation, we must.

TRY THIS! A TASTE FROM OUR CULTURE...

Peach Cobbler

Ingredients:
4 Cups peeled and sliced ripe peaches
2/3 Cup plus 3 tablespoons granulated sugar
1 teaspoon grated lemon zest
1 tablespoon fresh lemon juice
1/4 tablespoon almond extract
1 1/2 Cups unbleached all-purpose flour
1 tablespoon baking powder
1/2 tablespoon salt
1/3 Cup vegetable shortening
1 egg, lightly beaten
1/4 Cup milk
1 Cup heavy cream, chilled
3 to 4 tablespoons peach brandy or peach cordial

Method:
1. Preheat oven to 400° F. Butter a 2-quart baking dish.
2. Arrange peaches in a baking dish. Sprinkle with 2/3 cup sugar, the lemon zest and juice, and almond extract.
3. Bake for 20 minutes.
4. While peaches are baking, sift the flour, 1 tablespoon of the remaining sugar, the baking powder and salt together into a bowl. Cut in shortening until mixture resembles cornmeal. Combine beaten egg and milk and mix into dry ingredients until just combined.
5. Remove peaches from oven and quickly drop dough by large spoonfuls over surface. Sprinkle with remaining 2 tablespoons sugar. Return to the oven for 15 0r 20 minutes, until top is firm and golden brown.
6. Whip cream to soft peaks. Flavor with peach brandy to taste.
7. Serve cobbler warm, accompanied by whipped cream.
Makes 4 to 6 portions

CHAPTER 15 FRANCE

A LOOK UPON

Look upon the world

and see,

bitterness and strife.

Look upon the world

and see,

many, a horrible life.

Look upon a war-torn field,

See a blooming daffodil.

Its petals bright

Its green stem strong

It thrives

It survives

It's me.

France

Population 56.6 million

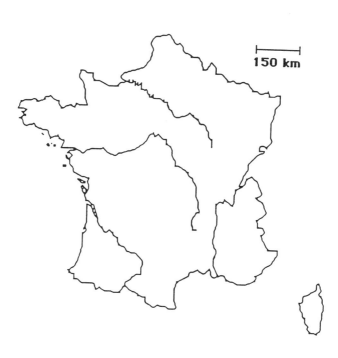

WHERE DO I BELONG

On a clear evening, I can sometimes see the faint lights from the Eiffel Tower from the rooftop of our dingy apartment building on the outskirts of Paris. With mixed emotions, I ponder over who and what I am. I know I am sixteen. I know I am the youngest daughter of Turkish immigrants. I know my parents are fundamentalist Muslims. My skin is dark and swarthy and my hair is shiny black. My eyes are almond shaped and bright, and I have lived in this ghetto in France with Algerians, Moroccans, Arabs, and Africans all of my life. This is what I know. I have been educated in French schools. I act and speak French. I know the French language and culture much more than my Turkish heritage. My schooling has been excellent and my grades the same, but somehow I feel I do not belong anywhere.

I want to fit into French society, the land I have known all my life, but it is difficult. I look different. I do not look French and that singles me out. Sometimes my friends and I walk some of the streets of Paris at night and we are always stopped by the police. They ask us for our papers, but we are doing nothing wrong. We are just in the wrong side of town at night.

Most immigrants live in the ghettos in France. It is here we are told to speak French and be French because it is not a multicultural society here. The government does not tolerate religious difference or cultures. We practice our Muslim religion in secrecy because the people here just would not understand our way. Some have been expelled from school for their cultural and religious differences.

That is my problem. I am not accepted as being French because I am a Turkish immigrant. As I am here, I lose my Turkish heritage day by day. To make matters worse, I am dating a French boy.

No, my parents do not know and his parents do not know. My parents want me to marry a Turkish boy. Where am I supposed to find him, eh? His parents want him to marry the finest French girl but, I am glad to know that Jacques loves me for who I am. It doesn't matter that I am Turkish. He makes me feel happy. I feel I belong with him. We hope to go to a university together and then get married someday.

I understand that the immigration laws of France are changing. Soon the doors of all immigration will be closed. Fewer immigrants are being allowed to stay in France because the government does not like a multicultural society and because they are afraid of becoming anything less than French.

So this is my life as a "beur" here. All immigrants are called beurs. I think people fear what they do not know. If only they would give us a chance. We are good people. We are hard-working people.

All of this makes me sad because I am a person , a good and nice person. Why can't people accept that? I have the best of two cultures. I am Amira, Turkish and French, and I continue to search for the place where I belong.

EXCERPTS FROM AN INTERVIEW

Donna Clovis: What struggles has the country of France had recently?

Annick: Last year and this year in 1994, the economy in France has been very bad. Young people who graduate from the university as well as those who do not, cannot find jobs. That's what all of the demonstrations in Paris have been about. Thousands of students are trying to get the governments attention to solve the situation.

DC: How serious is the situation?

Annick: It is quite serious. Without jobs or work, you cannot eat or get a place to live. Young people are beginning to panic over the situation.

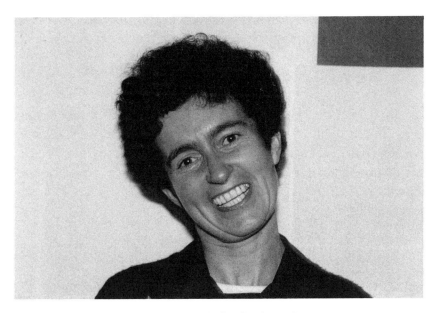

Annick smiles during her interview.

DC: Do you think things will get better?

Annick: Maybe. Only if the economy starts to get better.

DC: What do young people in France think of the United States?

Annick: They think the United States is a model for all to follow. They love sports, especially basketball. They don't have teams like these to join at school. They love the United States. They love its music too. The United States is a big brother to them.

DC: What do adults in France think of the United States?

Annick: Some older people are afraid of losing their French culture to the United States. For example, we have always used different English words as part of our everyday French conversation; like parking and stop and chewing gum. Now there are individuals who want to change these words into French words. I think it is a little ridiculous. You are not American if you use some English words or even if you speak English. I know I am proud I am French.

DC: What is your favorite place in France?

Annick: I love the Alps. They are the most beautiful and scenic places in the winter with the snow capped mountains. The air is crisp and clear. I love to take quiet walks there with my family. My other favorite place is Brittany. It is located by the sea. There's abundant wildlife like frogs and different birds. There are boats and spacious beaches.

DC: What's your favorite French food?

Annick: I love "blanquette." It's veal with a type of dressing on it.

DC: What are the schools like in France?

Annick: Children have very long school days in France. They go from 8:30 in the morning to 4:30. There are even classes on Saturday morning. Most students have at least one hour of homework. Those students in high school must study at least three hours a day. There are only two hours of gym per week and like I said there are no after school sports or play or clubs. I think school is very difficult for French children. They study English, Math, and History every day. We usually eat dinner by 7:30 or 8:00 after all the homework is done. Schools are also very poor. We don't have all of the computers like you have in the United States. We don't have as many materials or copying machines. You are very lucky here.

DC: What are the Universities like?

Annick: We don't have to pay for a college education like you do in the United States. It is all free and public. After high school, you can go there and graduate with a B.A. degree.

DC: What brings you to the United States?

Annick: My husband is here on business. He is an engineer and we have been here five years. I am a teacher. We plan to go back to France this year. Our family has had a great time here. I'm glad we had the opportunity to be in America.

TRY THIS! A TASTE FROM OUR CULTURE...
Bûche de Noël (French)

Ingredients:
1 box angel-food cake mix
2 C chocolate frosting
1/4 C icing sugar
decorations such as marzipan mushrooms

Method:
1. Line 2 cookie sheets, the type with edges all around, with waxed paper. Grease and flour the paper well.
2. Prepare the cake mix as directed. Pour half of the batter into each pan. Bake at 350° F for 20-25 minutes.
3. Immediately turn out each cake, top down, onto a peice of waxed paper that is liberally sprinkled with icing sugar. Remove the lining paper and trim off any crusty edges. While the cakes are still hot, roll up each one from the short end with the waxed paper. Place each cake, seam side down, on a rack to cool.
4. When the cakes are completely cool, unroll them. Take one third of the frosting and divide it into two portions. Spread one portion evenly and thinly on one cake. Spread the other portion on the other cake.
5. Roll up each cake without the waxed paper. To make one long log, place the cakes end to end and seam side down on a tray. Cover with the remaining frosting. Use the blade of a knife or the tines of a fork to make a bark pattern in the icing.
6. Sprinkle icing "snow" on top. Decorate with marzipan mushrooms. Cut into slices, each one having a ring pattern similar to that of a real log.

CONCLUSION

PRAYER

May freedom always prosper in the heart of humanity

May our visions blossom like clouds and surpass heights of sky

May we grow in knowledge and acceptance of others

May we learn to love

Cease to hate

Unite in strength